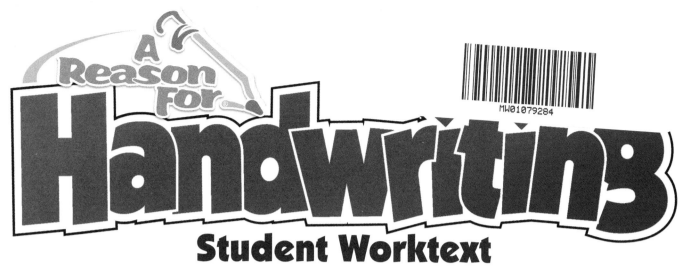

Student Worktext

Cursive C

ISBN#: 0-936785-41-1
TL#: HWSWTC2012

Published by The Concerned Group, Inc.
700 East Granite • P.O. Box 1000 • Siloam Springs, AR 72761

Authors Carol Ann Retzer, Eva Hoshino
Publisher Russ L. Potter, II
Project Director Kristin Potter
Senior Editor Bill Morelan
Creative Director Daniel Potter
Research Asst. Marklyn Retzer
Proofreader Rachel Tucker
Illustrations Rob Harrell & Josh Ray
Colorists Josh & Aimee Ray

Scripture translation selected for appropriate vocabulary level.
All verses are taken from *The Living Bible*, Tyndale House Publishers,
Wheaton, Illinois 60187. Used by permission.

Printed in the United States on recyclable paper

For more information about A Reason For Handwriting®, A Reason For Spelling®,
A Reason For Science®, & A Reason For Guided Reading®, write to the address
above or visit our website.

www.AReasonFor.com

Please, Help Us Hold Down Costs!

Photocopy machines are wonderful inventions, but did you know that it's ILLEGAL to reproduce copyrighted material?

Years of work and hundreds of thousands of dollars have gone into the development and production of **A Reason For Handwriting**®. Only your Christian integrity can help us avoid unnecessary price increases due to ILLEGAL photocopying.

Thank you for honoring copyright laws and not yielding to the temptation to "run off a few copies." It's not cost effective and it's ILLEGAL as well!

Attention Parents & Teachers:

Don't Settle for HALF a Curriculum!

A Reason For Handwriting® Student Worktexts integrate faith and learning by featuring lessons based on Scripture verses and built-in opportunities for sharing God's Word with others.

But, the **A Reason For Handwriting®** curriculum offers much, much more!

The **Comprehensive K-6th Teacher Guidebook** is full of essential instructions, helpful tips, and teacher-tested techniques to help you make the most of your handwriting practice.

Key instructional information in the **Teacher Guidebook** includes:

- **The Suggested Weekly Schedule**
- **Daily Lesson Plans**
- **Tips for Teaching Cursive Handwriting**
- **Techniques for Grading**

Plus the **Teacher Guidebook** includes a wealth of teacher-tested tips and enrichment ideas:

- **A Comprehesive Skills Index**
- **Extended Activities**
- **Ways to Share Border Sheets**
- **Letter Formation Charts**
- **Tips for Proper Positioning**
- **Letter Group Charts**
- **Vocabulary Lists**
- **Common Handwriting Problems**
- **Black Line Masters**

To order the **A Reason For Handwriting®** K-6th Teacher Guidebook that goes with this **Student Worktext**, contact your curriculum supplier or call 800.447.4332

Or go to:
www.areasonfor.com

Just For Kids!

Welcome to A Reason For Handwriting®

This year you'll learn to write better, memorize Scripture, share God's Word, and have FUN!

Each week you'll practice letters and groups of letters from a different Scripture verse. Then you'll write the entire verse on practice paper. At the end of each week you'll pick a Scripture Border Sheet from the back of your Worktext,

Parker

Susan

Rodney

write the verse in your very best handwriting, and use your creative talents to color and decorate it. Now comes the really FUN part: Sharing God's Word!

You can share God's Word, in your very own handwriting, by giving people your finished Scripture Border Sheets! You can take them to nursing homes, share them with friends, make placemats for your kitchen table, mail them to someone who isn't feeling well. . . you get the idea. And we're sure you'll come up with even more ideas throughout the year!

And sharing God's Word with others gives you the very best reason for improving your handwriting!

Meet New Friends

Throughout this book, you'll see illustrations of kids like you who are caring, sharing, working, and learning. Be sure to watch for these new faces!

How to Become A Five Star Student!

Do you want your writing to look its very best? Here are the five basic areas you should consider when evaluating your handwriting form:

Alignment
Each letter or word should sit on the line, not above or below it.

Slant
The letter slant should be uniform and consistent. (To help you determine slant, draw a top-to-bottom line straight down the middle of each letter in a sentence.)

Size
Capital letters are all one full space tall. The lowercase letters *b, d, f, h, k, l,* and *t* are also one space tall. All other lowercase letters are half-a-space tall. Also, any letter that goes below the line should extend for half a space.

Shape
Letters should be consistent and easy to read. Minor differences from the model are okay, but all your letters must be formed with the proper strokes to avoid developing bad habits.

Spacing
Letters should be clearly identifiable. They should not run into each other, or be too far apart. Each word should be separated from the next word. Remember, a little more space is needed between sentences than between words.

Follow these guidelines, focusing on consistency and quality, and you'll be a **Five Star** student!

The following practice sentence contains all the letters of the alphabet:

God created zebras and foxes to walk, jump, and hide very quickly.

Notes To The Teacher

As students begin these Daily Letter Practice Review Lessons, it's important to help them discover the similarities and differences between the Manuscript and Cursive versions of each letter. This activity helps students form clear mental models of letters and strokes, leading to more accurate letter formation and better handwriting.

Also, many letters in cursive writing use similar patterns in their formation. Be sure to emphasize these similarities by using the information found in the Cursive Letter Groups (Teacher Guidebook page 234). This will greatly enhance student understanding as you introduce new letters.

Daily Letter Practice Lessons 1 through 5 introduce the vowels. Since vowels are the most commonly used letters, it's important to master them thoroughly at the start. Lessons 6 through 26 cover all the remaining letters in alphabetical order. Lesson 27 reviews the entire alphabet and pages 36 & 37 allow for post-testing. Beginning on page 38, you'll find the weekly cursive lessons which review all capital and lowercase letters during the rest of the school year.

Practice Your Name

Ā ā   A a

A a

Ā   a

a

ā   a

a

ā a a   a a a

a a a

9

Practice Your Name

$\tilde{E}e$ $\mathcal{E}e$

$\mathcal{E}e$

$\tilde{\mathcal{E}}$ $\mathcal{E}$

$\mathcal{E}$

e

e

eee

eee

Practice Your Name

Practice Your Name

Oo   Oo   Ò o   Ò o   Ò o   Ò o

Oo

O   O

O

o   o

o

ooo   ooo

ooo

 **Focus Letter** Uu 𝒰𝓊

Practice Your Name

𝒰𝓊 𝒰𝓊

𝒰𝓊

𝒰 𝒰

𝒰

𝓊 𝓊

𝓊

𝓊𝓊𝓊𝓊𝓊 𝓊𝓊𝓊𝓊𝓊

𝓊𝓊𝓊𝓊𝓊

Practice Your Name → Brianna   Brianna

Bb Bb Bb Bb Bb Bb

Bb Bb Bb Bb Bb Bb

Bb Bb Bb Bb Bb Bb

B B B B B B B

B B B B B B B

B B B B B B B

b b b b b b b b b

b b b b b b b b b

b b b b b b b b b

b b b b b b b b

bbb bbb bbb bbb bbb bbb

bbb bbb bbb bbb bbb bbb

bbb bbb bbb bbb bbb bbb

Focus Letter: Cc Cc

Practice Your Name

Ĉĉ Cc

Cc

Ĉ C

C

ĉ c

c

ĉcc ccc

ccc

Practice Your Name

Dd Dd

Dd

D D

D

d d

d

ddd ddd

ddd

Focus Letter F f _Ff_

Practice Your Name

Practice Your Name

G g G g

G g

G g

G g

g g

g

ggg g g g

g g g

Focus Letter | Hh $\mathcal{H}h$

Practice Your Name

$\mathcal{H}h$ $\mathcal{H}h$

$\mathcal{H}h$

$\mathcal{H}$ $\mathcal{H}$

$\mathcal{H}$

h h

h

hhh hhh

hhh

Focus Letter J j *J j*

Practice Your Name

20

Practice Your Name

$\mathcal{K}k \quad \mathcal{K}k$

$\mathcal{K}k$

$\mathcal{K} \quad \mathcal{K}$

$\mathcal{K}$

$k \quad k$

k

$kkk \quad kkk$

kkk

Practice Your Name

$\mathcal{L}$ l

$\mathcal{L}$

$\mathcal{L}$

$\mathcal{L}$

l

l

lll

lll

Practice Your Name

𝓜𝓂 𝓜𝓂

𝓜𝓂

𝓜 𝓜

𝓜

𝓂 𝓂

𝓂

𝓂𝓂𝓂 𝓂𝓂𝓂

𝓂𝓂𝓂

Focus Letter Nn *𝒩𝓃*

Practice Your Name

𝒩𝓃 𝒩𝓃

𝒩𝓃

𝒩 𝒩

𝒩

𝓂 𝓂

𝓂

𝓂𝓃𝓃 𝓂𝓃𝓃

𝓂𝓃𝓃

Focus Letter Pp *Pp*

Practice Your Name

𝒫 p   𝒫 p

𝒫 p

𝒫   𝒫

𝒫

p   p

p

ppp   ppp

ppp

Practice Your Name

Q q Q q

Q q

Q Q

Q

q q

q

q q q q q q

q q q

Practice Your Name

Rr Rr

Rr

R R

R

r r

r

rrr rrr

rrr

Focus Letter Ss Ss

Practice Your Name

S s Ss

Ss

S S

S

s s

s

sss sss

sss

Practice Your Name

Practice Your Name

Practice Your Name

Ww Ww

Ww

U U

U

w w

w

www wuw

wuw

Practice Your Name

$\mathcal{X}\ \mathcal{X}x\quad \mathcal{X}x$

$\mathcal{X}x$

$\mathcal{X}\quad \mathcal{X}$

$\mathcal{X}$

$x\quad x$

x

$xxxx\quad xxx$

xxx

Focus Letter Yy Yy

Practice Your Name

Yy ny   Yy ny
Yy ny

Yy   Yy
Y

ny   ny
ny

nyyy   nyyy
nyyy

 **Focus Letter** Zz Zz

Practice Your Name

Practice Lesson 27

Practice Your Name

$\bar{A}\bar{a}$ Bb $\hat{C}c$ Dd $\hat{E}e$ Ff Gg

Hh Ii Jj Kk Ll Mm

Nn Oo Pp Qq Rr Ss Tt

Uu Vv Ww Xx Yy Zz

1 2 3 4 5 6 7 8 9 0

Practice Your Name

Practice Your Name

To The Teacher

Before beginning instruction, please review the
Weekly Lesson Format (Teacher Guidebook, page 56).

You'll also find detailed directions for implementing
the 5-day format, as well as suggestions for using the
Scripture Border Sheets.

Careful review of this material at the start of the school year
will greatly enhance the effectiveness of this curriculum.

Name _____

TIP OF THE WEEK

As you get taller and smarter this year, make sure
your handwriting grows too! Strive to be a Five Star student.
(See page 6.) Good handwriting helps others read what you have to say.

Day One Practice the following letters and words from this week's Scripture.

Dd

doing

good

Make

Day Two Continue practicing letters and words from this week's Scripture.

Oo

opportunity

for

most

Day Three
Practice the final letters and words from this week's Scripture.

Yy

every

you

have

Day Four
Practice this week's entire Scripture verse by tracing over each of the words below.

Make the most of every opportunity you have for doing good.

Ephesians 5:16

FOR DISCUSSION
What are some "opportunities for doing good" you might find at school? Try to make the most of at least one opportunity this week.

Name_____

TIP OF THE WEEK

Close your eyes and picture the strokes for the capital
and lowercase a a, E e, and J j. With your eyes still closed,
write these six letters with your index finger on the palm of your other hand.

Day One Practice the following letters and words from this week's Scripture.

A a

Always

name

thanks

Day Two Continue practicing letters and words from this week's Scripture.

E e

Ephesians

everything

Father

Day Three
Practice the final letters and words from this week's Scripture.

Jj

Jesus

give

our

Day Four
Practice this week's entire Scripture verse by tracing over each of the words below.

Always give thanks for everything to our God and Father in the name of our Lord Jesus Christ.

Ephesians 5:20

FOR DISCUSSION

Make a list of things you are thankful for. Now compare your list with a friend's. How are they similar? How are they different?

TIP OF THE WEEK

Letters are different heights, just like people! Some
lowercase letters fill only half the space, while tall letters
(*b, d, f, h, k, l,* and *t*) fill the whole space, and touch the top lines.

Day One   Practice the following letters and words from this week's Scripture.

Rr

righteous

power

prayer

Day Two   Continue practicing letters and words from this week's Scripture.

Tt

The

earnest

great

Day Three   Practice the final letters and words from this week's Scripture.

Uu

results

wonderful

man

Day Four   Practice this week's entire Scripture verse by tracing over each of the words below.

The earnest prayer of a righteous man has great power and wonderful results.

James 5:16

FOR DISCUSSION
Does God always answer prayers with a "yes?" What other answers might God give? Why?

Name _____

TIP OF THE WEEK

When you tie your shoes, you make loops for the bows.
When you write some letters, you make loops, too! Make certain
the loops in *b, e, f, h, k,* and *l* are open — but don't put loops in *t* or *d*.

Day One   Practice the following letters and words from this week's Scripture.

L l

Lord

glad

the

Day Two   Continue practicing letters and words from this week's Scripture.

P p

happens

friends

in

Day Three   Practice the final letters and words from this week's Scripture.

Ww

Whatever

be

dear

Day Four   Practice this week's entire Scripture verse by tracing over each of the words below.

Whatever happens, dear friends,
be glad in the Lord.
Philippians 3:1

FOR DISCUSSION
Is it possible to be "glad in the Lord" even when you're having a bad day? Explain.

Name _____

TIP OF THE WEEK

The capitals *G* and *S* are "boatstroke" capitals.
The other boatstroke capitals are *B, F, I,* and *T.*
Remember, boatstroke capitals are not joined to the rest of the word.

Day One   Practice the following letters and words from this week's Scripture.

Gg

God

ago

Long

Day Two   Continue practicing letters and words from this week's Scripture.

Ss

chose

us

own

Day Three
Practice the final letters and words from this week's Scripture.

Vv

very

even

world

Day Four
Practice this week's entire Scripture verse by tracing over each of the words below.

Long ago, even before He made the world, God chose us to be His very own.

Ephesians 1:4

FOR DISCUSSION
How does it make you feel that God has chosen you? How should this relationship affect your behavior? Be specific.

TIP OF THE WEEK

Is your hand getting tired as you write? You may
be holding your pencil incorrectly, or too tightly. Have your
teacher check your pencil position. Relax your wrist by rotating it in a circle.

Day One Practice the following letters and words from this week's Scripture.

Bb

Because

done

that

Day Two Continue practicing letters and words from this week's Scripture.

Cc

Christ

become

gifts

Day Three Practice the final letters and words from this week's Scripture.

Hh

He

what

delights

Day Four Practice this week's entire Scripture verse by tracing over each of the words below.

Because of what Christ has done, we have become gifts to God that He delights in.

Ephesians 1:11

FOR DISCUSSION
Is a gift always an object, or can our actions be a gift, too? Name some gifts that you might share with God.

50

Name_____

📖 **TIP OF THE WEEK**

There are four lowercase letters (*i, j, t,*
and *x*) that require an extra stroke after the word
is written. Pay close attention to these letters as you practice.

Day One Practice the following letters and words from this week's Scripture.

Ii

If

lies

lips

Day Two Continue practicing letters and words from this week's Scripture.

Kk

keep

happy

guard

Day Three — Practice the final letters and words from this week's Scripture.

Tt

telling

tongue

control

Day Four — Practice this week's entire Scripture verse by tracing over each of the words below.

If you want a happy, good life, keep control of your tongue, and guard your lips from telling lies.

I Peter 3:10

FOR DISCUSSION

Everyone knows that lying is wrong. But are there other ways that the things we say might cause problems? Explain.

The bridgestroke family includes
the lowercase *b*, *o*, *v* and *w*. As you
write the connecting stroke, don't let your bridge sag!

Day One Practice the following letters and words from this week's Scripture.

Ff

following

full

of

Day Two Continue practicing letters and words from this week's Scripture.

Vv

love

loved

Who

Day Three
Practice the final letters and words from this week's Scripture.

Xx

example

exciting

others

Day Four
Practice this week's entire Scripture verse by tracing over each of the words below.

Be full of love for others,
following the example of Christ
Who loved you.
Ephesians 5:2

FOR DISCUSSION
List some ways you can show your love for your family. . .your friends. . .your neighbors.

Tip of the Week

A train won't work unless it's on
the track. Keep your handwriting on track this
week by making sure your letters rest firmly on the line.

Day One — Practice the following letters and words from this week's Scripture.

A a

Always

again

say

Day Two — Continue practicing letters and words from this week's Scripture.

J j

joy

rejoice

coming

Day Three — Practice the final letters and words from this week's Scripture.

Rr

Remember

Lord

soon

Day Four — Practice this week's entire Scripture verse by tracing over each of the words below.

Always be full of joy in the
Lord; I say it again, rejoice!...
Remember that the Lord is
coming soon.

Philippians 4:4,5

FOR DISCUSSION

Look up Psalms 118:24. How is it similar to this week's verse? How is it different?

Name _____

📘 **TIP OF THE WEEK**

This verse contains most of the overstroke letters
(*m, n, v, w*). Think of some words that contain the
other overstroke letters (*x* and *y*) and practice them, too!

Day One Practice the following letters and words from this week's Scripture.

Mm

Most

important

makes

Day Two Continue practicing letters and words from this week's Scripture.

Nn

continue

many

deep

Day Three — Practice the final letters and words from this week's Scripture.

Oo

other

show

faults

Day Four — Practice this week's entire Scripture verse by tracing over each of the words below.

Most important of all, continue
to show deep love for each other,
for love makes up for many of
your faults.

I Peter 4:8

FOR DISCUSSION

Why is it so important for Christians to love one another? (Hint: see John 13:34, 35.)

Name _____

Just like the capital *C*, the oval capital *E* begins just below
the top line. Also, remember that the forward oval capitals *B, P,*
and *R* begin with a flagstroke. (Notice the flagpole is leaning a bit!)

Day One   Practice the following letters and words from this week's Scripture.

Ee

each

given

abilities

Day Two   Continue practicing letters and words from this week's Scripture.

Pp

Peter

help

special

Day Three — Practice the final letters and words from this week's Scripture.

Ss

some

sure

use

Day Four — Practice this week's entire Scripture verse by tracing over each of the words below.

God has given each of you some special abilities; be sure to use them to help each other.

I Peter 4:10

FOR DISCUSSION

What special ability, knowledge, or talent has God given you? List some things that all of us can do to be helpful.

Name _____

TIP OF THE WEEK

The *H*, *J*, and *K*, are two-stroke capital letters.
There is also one three-stroke capital letter. Can you guess
what it is? (Here's a hint: It's just like a *J*, but with one stroke more.)

Day One Practice the following letters and words from this week's Scripture.

Hh

His

their

prayers

Day Two Continue practicing letters and words from this week's Scripture.

Ll

Lord

children

listening

Day Three
Practice the final letters and words from this week's Scripture.

It

The

to

watching

Day Four
Practice this week's entire Scripture verse by tracing over each of the words below.

The Lord is watching His children, listening to their prayers.
I Peter 3:12

FOR DISCUSSION

Having someone watch us can make us feel very good. But sometimes it makes us feel bad. What are some possible reasons for this?

TIP OF THE WEEK

The lowercase *g* and *q* are very similar. Be certain you
know which way the tail goes for each. The *q* is usually found
beside its best friend, the *u*. Practice the *qu* combination this week.

Day One Practice the following letters and words from this week's Scripture.

Bb

Be

beautiful

inside

Day Two Continue practicing letters and words from this week's Scripture.

Gg

gentle

lasting

precious

Day Three — Practice the final letters and words from this week's Scripture.

Qq

quiet

spirit

charm

Day Four — Practice this week's entire Scripture verse by tracing over each of the words below.

Be beautiful inside, in your
hearts, with the lasting charm of
a gentle and quiet spirit which is
so precious to God.

I Peter 3:4

FOR DISCUSSION

Can someone be pretty on the outside, but ugly on the inside? How about the opposite? Explain.

Name _____

TIP OF THE WEEK

Everyone's name is special. You may be named
after a relative, or family friend, or something totally unique!
Be proud of your name and write it so anyone can read it!

Day One   Practice the following letters and words from this week's Scripture.

Oo

loving

one

toward

Day Two   Continue practicing letters and words from this week's Scripture.

Uu

humble

should

tender

Day Three
Practice the final letters and words from this week's Scripture.

Yy

family

sympathy

minds

Day Four
Practice this week's entire Scripture verse by tracing over each of the words below.

You should be like one big
happy family, full of sympathy
toward each other, loving one
another with tender hearts and
humble minds.

I Peter 3:8

FOR DISCUSSION
When someone you care about feels bad, do you feel bad, too? How does this relate to our Scripture verse this week?

Name _____

TIP OF THE WEEK

There are two dotted letters this week — the *i* and *j*.
Add a small dot (not a circle) after you finish the word. Also,
check your lowercase *e*'s to make sure they don't look like *i*'s.

Day One Practice the following letters and words from this week's Scripture.

Ff

fellowship

wonderful

we

Day Two Continue practicing letters and words from this week's Scripture.

Ii

If

light

living

Day Three — Practice the final letters and words from this week's Scripture.

Jj

John

joy

presence

Day Four — Practice this week's entire Scripture verse by tracing over each of the words below.

If we are living in the light of God's presence... we have wonderful fellowship and joy with each other.

— I John 1:7

FOR DISCUSSION

According to this verse, how does our relationship with God affect the way we relate to each other? Explain.

Lesson 16

TIP OF THE WEEK

Your lowercase oval letters (*a, c, d, g, o,* and *q*) should
be round and smooth, not squashed like someone sat on them!
To look its best, the oval part of each letter should fill the middle space.

Day One   Practice the following letters and words from this week's Scripture.

A a

snap

are

at

Day Two   Continue practicing letters and words from this week's Scripture.

Dd

Don't

unkind

evil

Day Three

Practice the final letters and words from this week's Scripture.

Rr

repay

those

back

Day Four

Practice this week's entire Scripture verse by tracing over each of the words below.

Don't repay evil for evil. Don't snap back at those who say unkind things about you... We are to be kind to others, and God will bless us for it.

— I Peter 3:9

FOR DISCUSSION

How should you act when someone is being unkind? What should our attitude be toward those who are mean to us? (Hint: see Luke 23:34.)

Name _____

TIP OF THE WEEK

Just as you need space between a classmate's desk and
your desk, words also need a letter space between them for easier reading.
Wordsthataretooclosetogether are much too hard to read!

Day One Practice the following letters and words from this week's Scripture.

Hh

home

within

that

Day Two Continue practicing letters and words from this week's Scripture.

Ss

hearts

as

trust

Day Three
Practice the final letters and words from this week's Scripture.

Uu

living

more

pray

Day Four
Practice this week's entire Scripture verse by tracing over each of the words below.

I pray that Christ will be
more and more at home in your
hearts, living within you as you
trust in Him.

Ephesians 3:17

FOR DISCUSSION
What does it mean to make someone
"feel at home?" Describe the kind of
heart where Jesus could feel at home.

Name _____

TIP OF THE WEEK

Look for similarities and differences between the
lowercase *u-w,* and the *m-n*. Make certain you write
these letters clearly and carefully so they can't be mistaken for each other.

Day One — Practice the following letters and words from this week's Scripture.

Nn

and

then

wants

Day Two — Continue practicing letters and words from this week's Scripture.

Pp

Philippians

helping

obey

Day Three
Practice the final letters and words from this week's Scripture.

Ww

want

work

what

Day Four
Practice this week's entire Scripture verse by tracing over each of the words below.

God is at work within you, helping you want to obey Him, and then helping you do what He wants.

Philippians 2:13

FOR DISCUSSION
Where does this verse say the desire to obey comes from? List some ways that we can become closer to God.

Name _____

TIP OF THE WEEK

Look for similarities and differences between
the lowercase *h* and *k*. Like the lowercase *u - w* and
m - n, these letters must be written clearly to avoid mistakes in reading.

Day One   Practice the following letters and words from this week's Scripture.

Bb

bring

be

child

Day Two   Continue practicing letters and words from this week's Scripture.

Gg

good

glory

which

Day Three   Practice the final letters and words from this week's Scripture.

Kk

kind

doing

praise

Day Four   Practice this week's entire Scripture verse by tracing over each of the words below.

May you always be doing those good, kind things which show that you are a child of God, for this will bring much praise and glory to the Lord.

Philippians 1:11

FOR DISCUSSION

List some ways we can help our neighbors. How does our kind behavior affect what people think about Christians?

Name _____

TIP OF THE WEEK

Have you looked at the "stars" lately? The Five Star
evaluation can help you determine areas in your handwriting
that need work. Watch your alignment, shape, size, slant and spacing.

Day One Practice the following letters and words from this week's Scripture.

Dd

grudges

ready

hold

Day Two Continue practicing letters and words from this week's Scripture.

Ee

Remember

gentle

never

Day Three Practice the final letters and words from this week's Scripture.

Ff

forgave

forgive

must

Day Four Practice this week's entire Scripture verse by tracing over each of the words below.

Be gentle and ready to forgive;
never hold grudges. Remember, the
Lord forgave you, so you must
forgive others.
Colossians 3:13

FOR DISCUSSION
How can holding a grudge be harmful?
Why do you think forgiving each
other is important?

Name _____

TIP OF THE WEEK

Some of us look a lot like our parents. Some
capital and lowercase pairs look alike, too. The *Cc* is
one such pair. Also look at the *Aa, Xx, Yy, Zz.*

Day One Practice the following letters and words from this week's Scripture.

Cc

Colossians

church

perfect

Day Two Continue practicing letters and words from this week's Scripture.

Ll

life

let

whole

Day Three
Practice the final letters and words from this week's Scripture.

Mm

Most

harmony

all

Day Four
Practice this week's entire Scripture verse by tracing over each of the words below.

Most of all, let love guide your life, for then the whole church will stay together in perfect harmony.

Colossians 3:14

FOR DISCUSSION

If you really love everyone, how might it affect your behavior? List some ways you can let love guide your life.

Name _____

TIP OF THE WEEK

To help you remember the correct strokes,
skywrite the capital letters from this lesson (*I, J,*
and *Q*) and see if a classmate can tell which one you're writing.

Day One   Practice the following letters and words from this week's Scripture.

Ii

first

loving

comes

Day Two   Continue practicing letters and words from this week's Scripture.

Jj

James

peace

pure

Day Three
Practice the final letters and words from this week's Scripture.

Qq

quiet

heaven

gentleness

Day Four
Practice this week's entire Scripture verse by tracing over each of the words below.

But the wisdom that comes
from heaven is first of all pure
and full of quiet gentleness. Then
it is peace-loving and courteous.
James 3:17

FOR DISCUSSION
Think of someone who seems "full of quiet gentleness." How do you think they became that kind of person?

Name _____

TIP OF THE WEEK

Check your posture. It's amazing how much of a
difference correct posture can make in your handwriting. Also,
make sure your paper is going the same direction as your writing arm.

Day One Practice the following letters and words from this week's Scripture.

Kk

making

make

other's

Day Two Continue practicing letters and words from this week's Scripture.

Uu

faults

because

each

Day Three — Practice the final letters and words from this week's Scripture.

Xx

exception

allowance

patient

Day Four — Practice this week's entire Scripture verse by tracing over each of the words below.

Be patient with each other,
making allowance for each other's
faults because of your love.
Ephesians 4:2

FOR DISCUSSION

Have you ever been impatient with someone, or critical? How can we learn to make allowances for another's weaknesses?

Name_____

TIP OF THE WEEK

The apostrophe *s* on *God's* means we belong to God —
we're part of God's family! You can share with the rest of God's family
by giving your Scripture Border Sheet this week to someone new.

Day One Practice the following letters and words from this week's Scripture.

Cc

Christian

country

belong

Day Two Continue practicing letters and words from this week's Scripture.

Yy
You

family

members

Day Three — Practice the final letters and words from this week's Scripture.

Zz
citizens

household

God's

Day Four — Practice this week's entire Scripture verse by tracing over each of the words below.

You are members of God's very own family, citizens of God's country, and you belong in God's household with every other Christian.

Ephesians 2:19

FOR DISCUSSION
Isn't it great to be part of God's family?
List some ways you can share
God's love with others.

LOW FAT
MILK
99¢

TIP OF THE WEEK

Make sure your letters are "planted" in the right space. Your tail letters need to touch the bottom line, and your tall letters need to reach the top line.

Day One Practice the following letters and words from this week's Scripture.

Mm

May

marvelous

high

Day Two Continue practicing letters and words from this week's Scripture.

Oo

down

soil

roots

Day Three   Practice the final letters and words from this week's Scripture.

Ww

how

wide

understand

Day Four   Practice this week's entire Scripture verse by tracing over each of the words below.

May your roots go down deep
into the soil of God's marvelous
love; and may you be able to feel
and understand...how long, how
wide, how deep, and how high His
love really is.

Ephesians 3:17-19

FOR DISCUSSION
What do you think this verse means when it says our "roots" should "go down deep" into God's love? Explain.

TIP OF THE WEEK

Remember, to help you write more rapidly
and smoothly, be sure to dot your *i*'s and cross your *t*'s
after you finish the entire word. The same is true for *j*'s and *x*'s, too.

Day One Practice the following letters and words from this week's Scripture.

Gg

God

bring

understanding

Day Two Continue practicing letters and words from this week's Scripture.

Rr

ever

deeper

from

Day Three — Practice the final letters and words from this week's Scripture.

Tt

Thessalonians

patience

into

Day Four — Practice this week's entire Scripture verse by tracing over each of the words below.

May the Lord bring you into an ever deeper understanding of the love of God and of the patience that comes from Christ.

II Thessalonians 3:5

FOR DISCUSSION

What have you learned about the love of God this year? Why not share your new insights with a friend?

TIP OF THE WEEK

Always look for the good in
each other. Trade papers with a classmate,
then point out each other's best letters and words.

Day One   Practice the following letters and words from this week's Scripture.

A a

about

against

law

Day Two   Continue practicing letters and words from this week's Scripture.

D d

do

dear

another

Day Three
Practice the final letters and words from this week's Scripture.

Zz

criticize

speak

brothers

Day Four
Practice this week's entire Scripture verse by tracing over each of the words below.

Don't criticize and speak evil about each other, dear brothers. If you do, you will be fighting against God's law of loving one another.

James 4:11

FOR DISCUSSION
Compare this verse with Ephesians 4:2 (see lesson 23). How are they different? How are they similar?

92

TIP OF THE WEEK

This would be a good week to check your writing
slant. Draw a line from top to bottom through each letter on
Day Two. Are your lines parallel? (One challenging letter is the capital 𝓛 .)

Day One **Practice the following letters and words from this week's Scripture.**

Ee

live

complete

encouragement

Day Two **Continue practicing letters and words from this week's Scripture.**

Ii

attitude

with

gives

Day Three Practice the final letters and words from this week's Scripture.

Nn

harmony

steadiness

Romans

Day Four Practice this week's entire Scripture verse by tracing over each of the words below.

May God who gives patience,
steadiness, and encouragement help
you to live in complete harmony
with each other—each with the
attitude of Christ toward the other.
Romans 15:5

FOR DISCUSSION

What are some ways you can promote harmony with your friends? Your family? Your neighbors? Explain.

Name _____

TIP OF THE WEEK

Many canestroke capitals are connected
to the rest of the word. They include the *H*
and *M* from this lesson — plus *K*, *N*, *U*, *X*, and *Y*.

Day One   Practice the following letters and words from this week's Scripture.

Hh

He

thanks

others

Day Two   Continue practicing letters and words from this week's Scripture.

Mm

mercy

much

them

Day Three Practice the final letters and words from this week's Scripture.

Pp

Pray

plead

upon

Day Four Practice this week's entire Scripture verse by tracing over each of the words below.

Pray much for others; plead for God's mercy upon them; give thanks for all He is going to do for them.

I Timothy 2:1

FOR DISCUSSION
Make of list of people who might need your prayers. Use it as a reminder as you pray this week.

Your name is the most important
word you write. As you write it on your papers
in every class, take extra time to write it carefully and clearly.

Day One Practice the following letters and words from this week's Scripture.

Bb

bountiful

supply

gladly

Day Two Continue practicing letters and words from this week's Scripture.

Kk

know

ask

tell

Day Three Practice the final letters and words from this week's Scripture.

Ww

wisdom

who

always

Day Four Practice this week's entire Scripture verse by tracing over each of the words below.

If you want to know what God wants you to do, ask Him, and He will gladly tell you, for He is always ready to give a bountiful supply of wisdom to all who ask Him.

James 1:5

FOR DISCUSSION

List some situations where you might need a bountiful supply of wisdom. How does God help us in times like these?

98

TIP OF THE WEEK

For something "extra" this week, write the
word *extra* several times. This provides good practice
making the *x*. Don't forget to cross the *x* after your write the word.

Day One   Practice the following letters and words from this week's Scripture.

Cc

richly

increasing

bless

Day Two   Continue practicing letters and words from this week's Scripture.

Ff

freedom

from

fear

Day Three Practice the final letters and words from this week's Scripture.

Xx

anxiety

extra

grant

Day Four Practice this week's entire Scripture verse by tracing over each of the words below.

May God bless you richly and grant you increasing freedom from all anxiety and fear.

I Peter 1:2

FOR DISCUSSION

How does knowing God help us deal with our fears? What is your greatest fear? Why not ask God to help you with it right now?

TIP OF THE WEEK

As you write this last verse, remember the Five Star
challenge (alignment, shape, size, slant and spacing). You've grown in
handwriting skills this year. God wants you to keep growing more like Him, too!

Day One   Practice the following letters and words from this week's Scripture.

Ll

Let

lives

growing

Day Two   Continue practicing letters and words from this week's Scripture.

Ss

strong

See

trust

Day Three Practice the final letters and words from this week's Scripture.

Vv

vigorous

overflow

thanksgiving

Day Four Practice this week's entire Scripture verse by tracing over each of the words below.

See that you go on growing in the Lord, and become strong and vigorous in the truth you were taught. Let your lives overflow with joy and thanksgiving for all He has done.

Colossians 2:7

FOR DISCUSSION
Choose two character traits we've discussed this year that you'd like to improve this summer. Don't forget to ask God to help you!

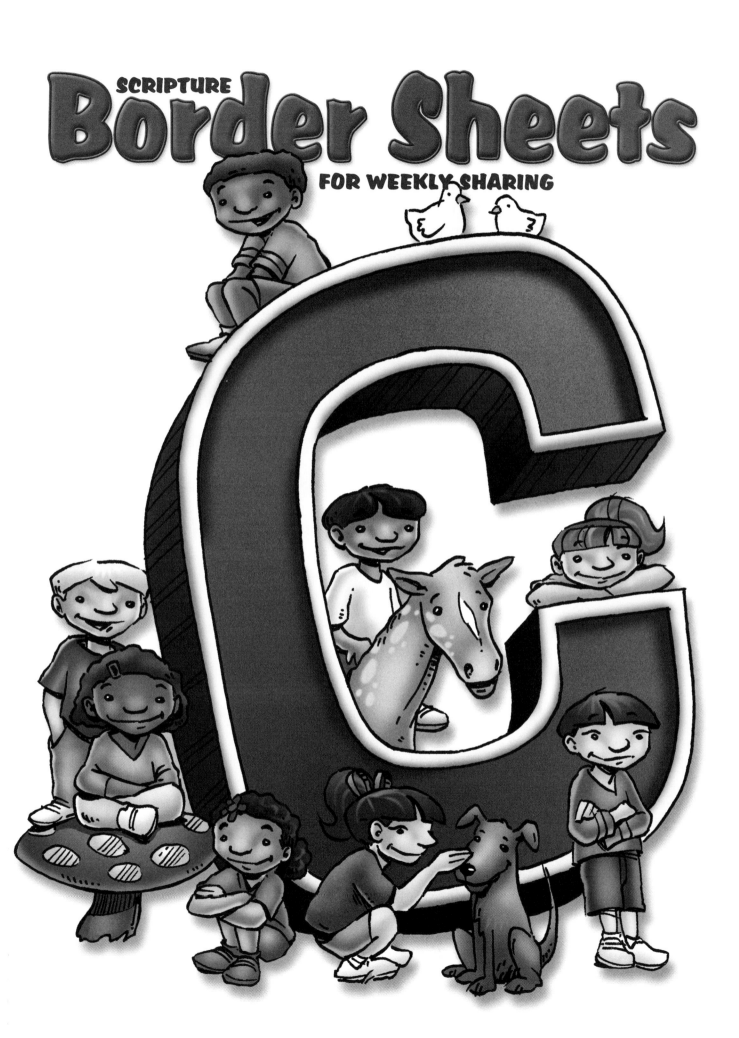

To The Teacher

The following pages are for use on Day 5 of the
Weekly Lesson Format (Teacher Guidebook, page 56).

These Scripture Border Sheets not only provide a
significant outreach component, but a strong
motivational tool as well.

This section contains 35 Scripture Border Sheets —
one per lesson, plus an extra, plus three blanks (pages
171–175) that allow for student-designed artwork.

For creative ways to use the Scripture Border Sheets
see "Ways to Share" (Teacher Guidebook, page 58).

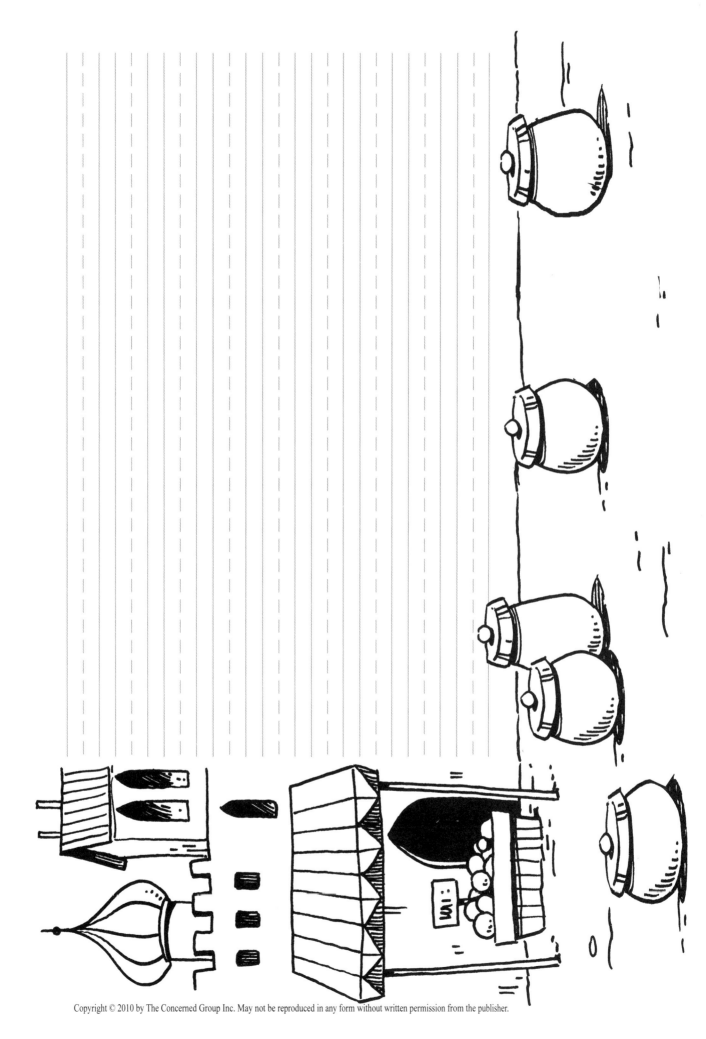

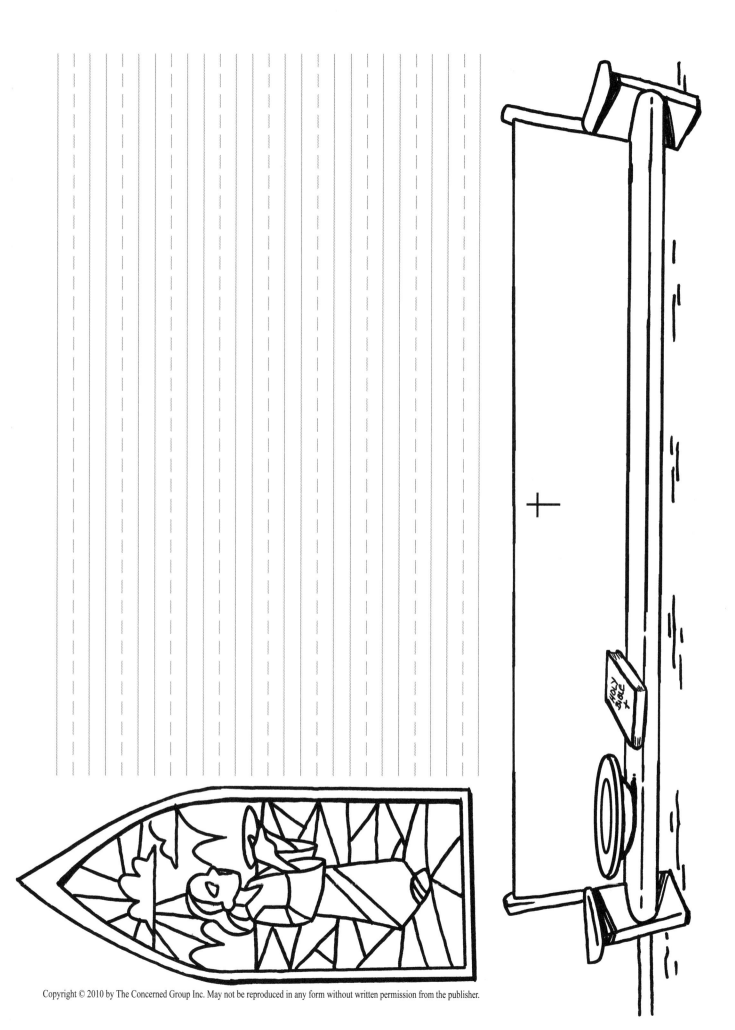

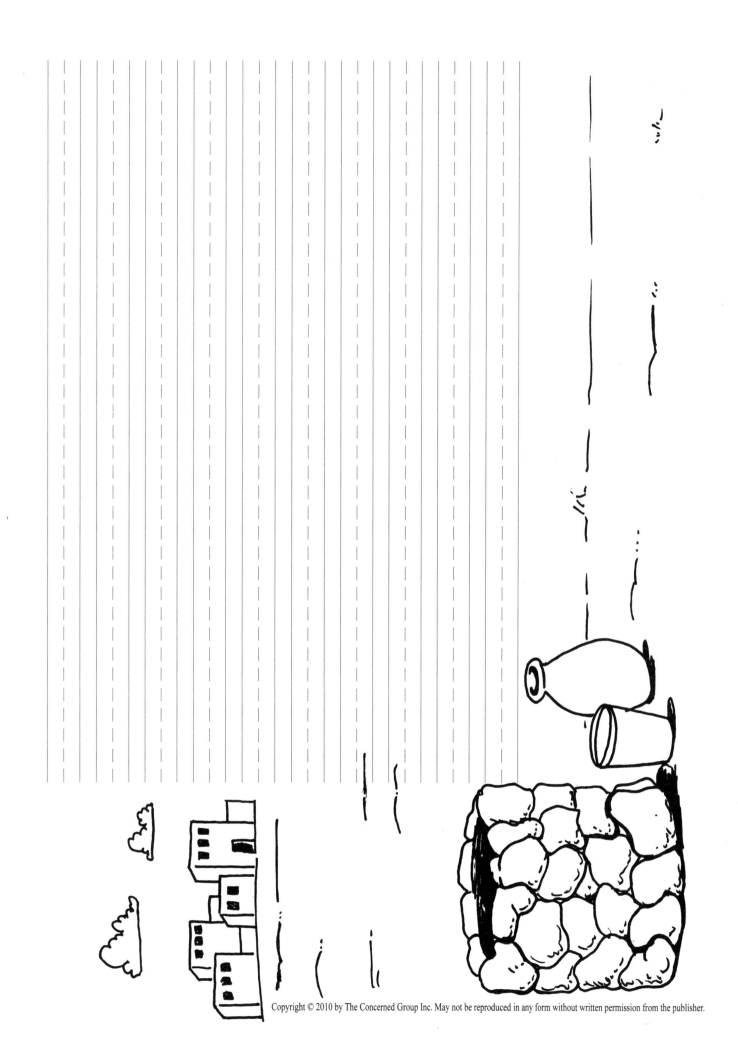

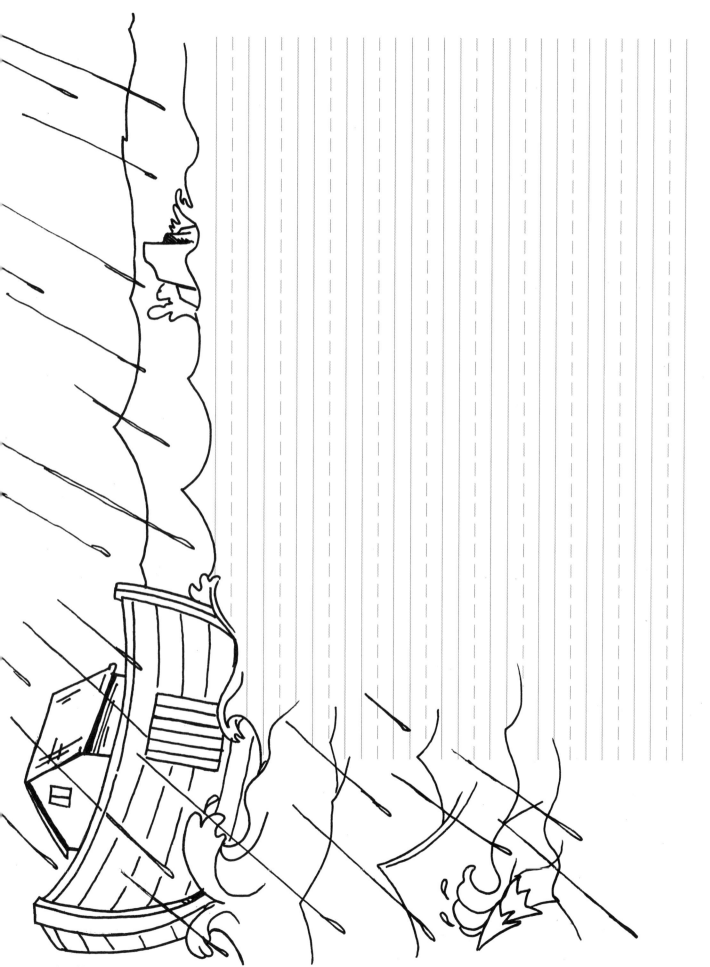

Salvation

Righteousness

Truth

READINESS

READINESS

FAITH

The WORD

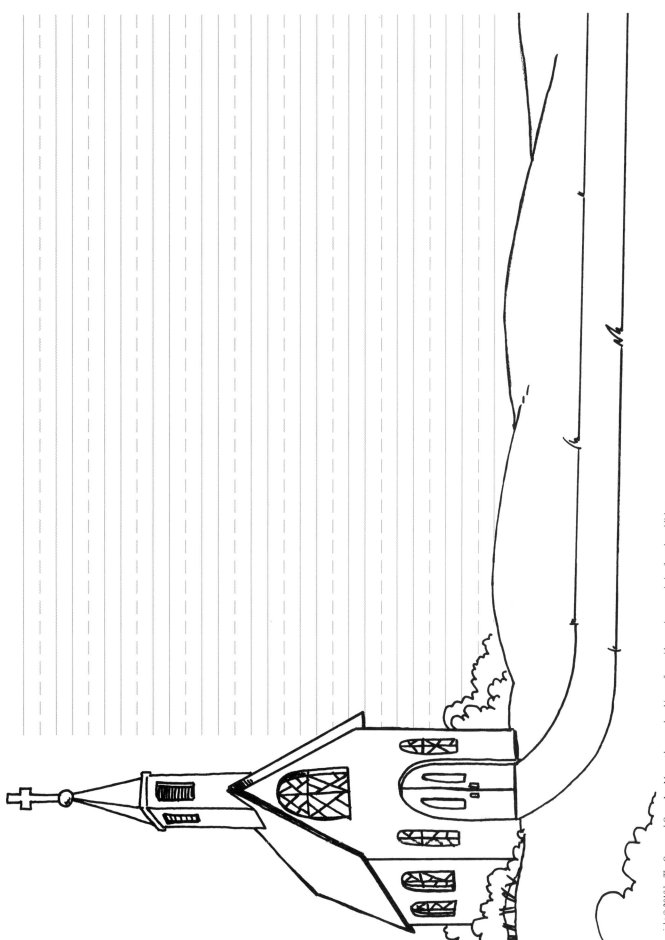

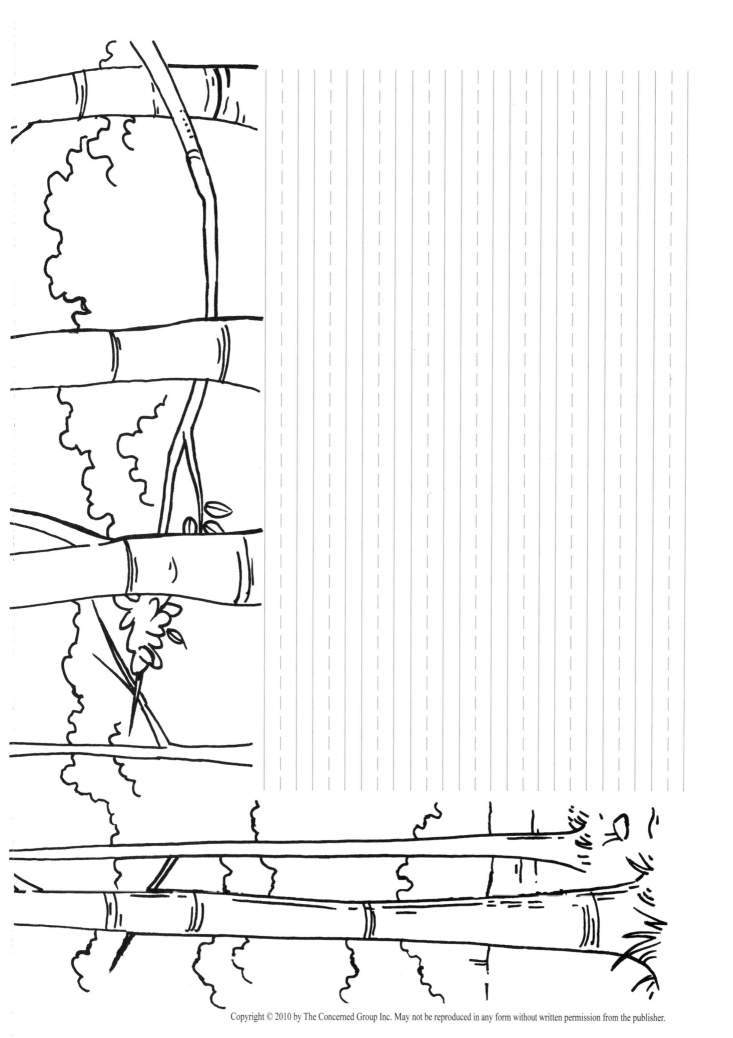

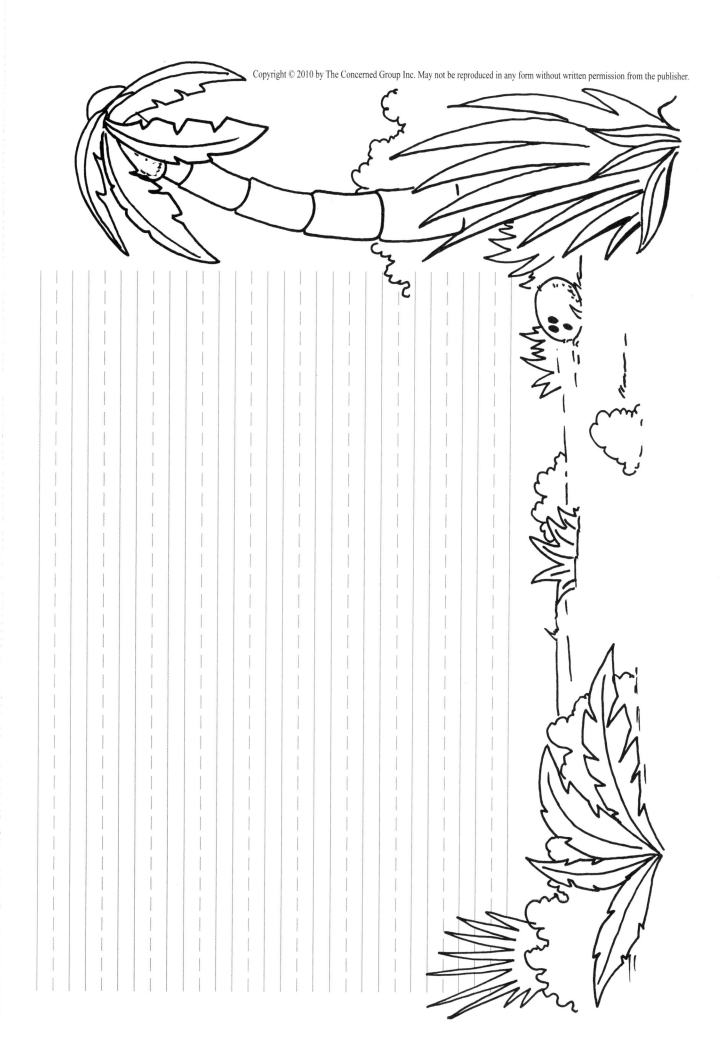

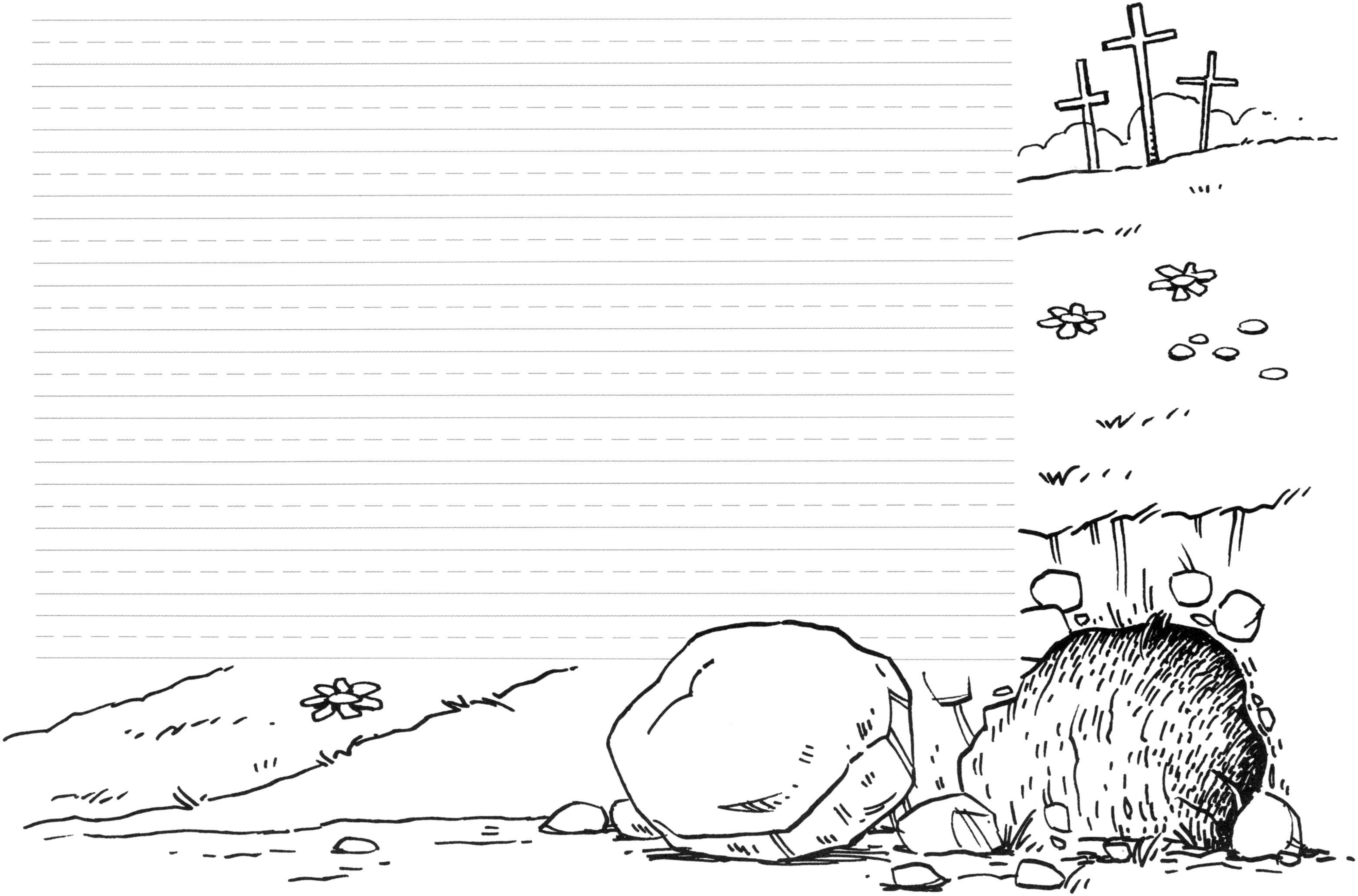

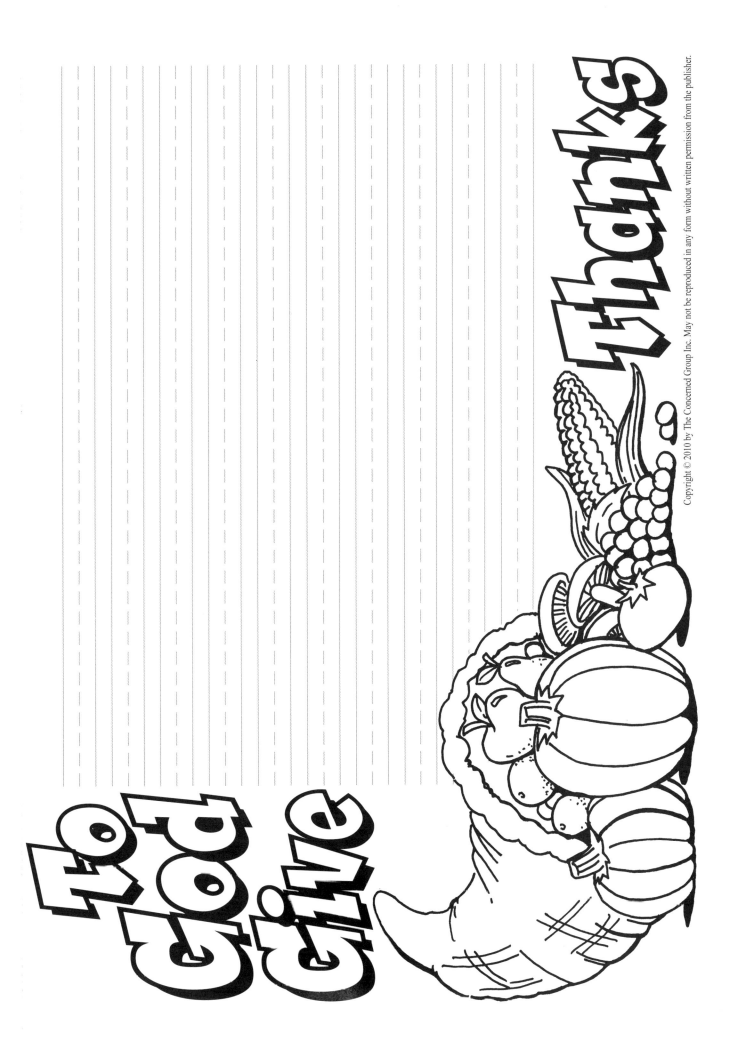

To God Give Thanks

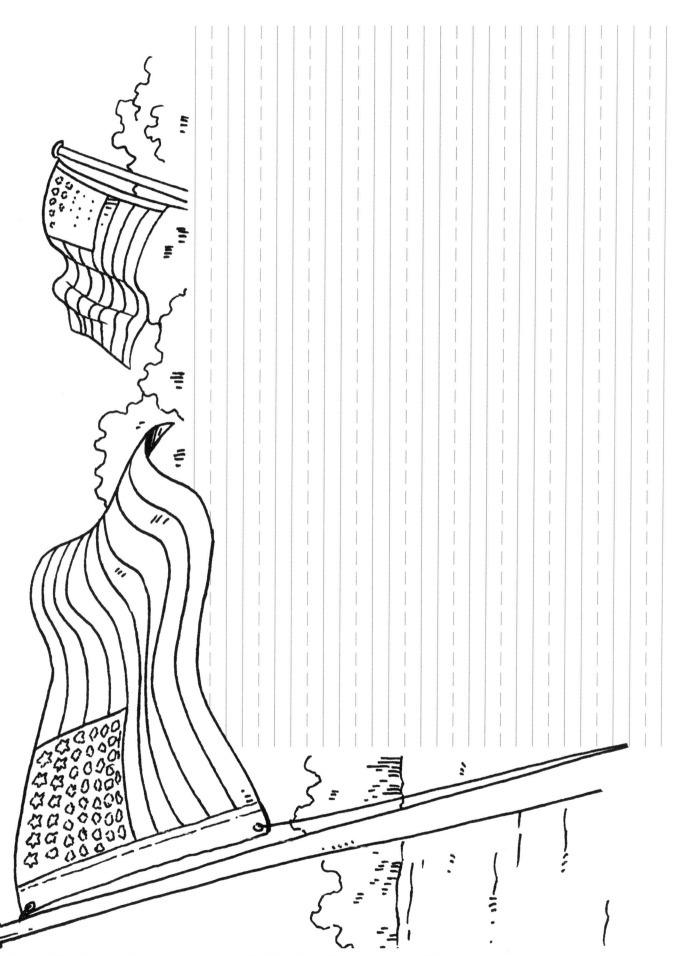